An Outdoor Educator's Guide to AWE

Understanding High Impact Learning

Kevin Long

AN OUTDOOR EDUCATOR'S
GUIDE TO AWE

Copyright © Kevin P. Long, August 2014

The Moral right of Kevin Long to be identified as the author of this work has been asserted in accordance with the Copyright, Design and Patents Act of 1988.

First Published 2015
The Outward Bound Trust
Hackthorpe Hall, Penrith, Cumbria CA10 2HX

ISBN-13: 978-0-9547782-1-7
ISBN-10: 0-9547782-1-9

A Catalogue record of this book is available
from the British Library

All Rights Reserved

Except for the quotation of short passages of criticism and review, no part of this book may be reproduced in any form, by photocopying or by any electronic or mechanical means, Including information storage or retrieval systems, without the prior written permission from both the copyright owner and the publisher of this book.

Printed and bound for

THE OUTWARD BOUND TRUST
www.outwardbound org.uk

An Outdoor Educator's Guide to AWE

"That life runs through our fingers
like water. We cannot stem the flow,
but we can drink deeply while it is there."

Seneca

For my son,
James.

PREFACE

The Outward Bound Trust is only too happy to endorse this book. Kevin Long has done a great job in identifying and exploring that special "something" that should lie at the heart of adventure and learning in the outdoors. The outdoor education sector has matured over the decades from an enterprising start-up into a fully evolved industry. Long ago you simply headed into the hills with a bunch of kids. Now it is regulated, measured, controlled and the subject of academic study with enough accompanying academic models to stretch from Ben Nevis to Scafell Pike. It is, of course, a sign of its importance, relevance and success that it has become so. But there is also the danger of leaching the magic from it all.

In the midst of this journey, we must not lose that which lies at the heart of outdoor learning – and "Awe" is as good a word as any to describe the concept. My seminal outdoor experience happened when, as a 13 year old, I was part of a school party going round the Snowdon Horseshoe. It was my first exposure to the British Hills and I found it beyond wonderful. Although I would not have used the word at the time, at supper in the hostel that night, I was awestruck. There is a direct line between that single outing and pretty much everything I have done since. Such is the power of awe.

And so it should be. Within The Outward Bound Trust we keep working hard to retain the awe of an adventure in the mountains because without this, it is merely healthy and worthy – and there are many other ways of being healthy and virtuous! I am proud that it is an Outward Bound® instructor who has stepped up to the plate and had the confidence and the insight to write this book.

Nick Barrett
Chief Executive
The Outward Bound Trust

December 2014

Contents

Part One – A Journey into Awesomeness... 1
    The Primeval Dawn... 2
    Tread Carefully... 5
    Understanding Awe... 6
    Heart of Reverence... 11
    A Catalyst for Caring... 13

Part Two –A Propensity To Be Awestruck... 18
    Awe Eliciting Experiences... 19
    The Power of Place... 24
    Reciprocity and Nature... 23
    Emotion and Purpose... 29
    Through The Eyes of A Child... 31
    Hold On To the Mystery... 35
    Receptiveness to Experience... 41
    Cultivating Awe-proneness... 46

Part Three – The Frame for Awe... 51
    The Power of Context... 52
    Address the Heart... 55
    Engaging With the Environment... 58
    Defamiliarisation- Seeing Anew... 62
    Framing & Awe Based Learning... 65
    Metaphor – Priming For Awe... 69
    Successful Outcomes... 72

Part Four – Magic Moments...	75
An Awescape...	77
Encounters with Awesomeness...	80
Evolving Themes of Awe...	84
On The Likelihood of Elicitors...	88
Part Five – Transformative Learning...	92
Interpretation of Unique Moments	93
Transformative Learning...	97
A Journey Within...	99
The Map Is Not the Territory...	102
Memory & The Effect of Frame...	106
The Experiencing Self...	108
The Beauty of Imperfection...	112
Appendix	115
Laboratory of Awe...	116
Acknowledgements	122
References	125
Index	130

Tables and Figures

Fig 1: Becoming Blinkered — 38
Fig 2.1: Student openness to learning and the Hierarchy of Needs — 41
Fig 2.2: Propensity to be Awestruck — 43
Fig 3: Categories of Awe — 47
Fig 4: Comparative Experiences — 53
Fig 5: The Rhys Six Box Model — 59
Fig 6: Schema Model of Understanding — 67
Fig 7: Effectiveness of Framing — 73
Fig 8: An AweScape — 76
Fig 9: From Peak Experiences to Awe — 83
Fig 10: Evolving Themes of Awe — 84
Fig 11: Frequency of Awe eliciting Experiences — 89
Fig 12: Informative v's Transformative learning — 98
Fig13: Roger's Personality Structure — 103

.....

FORWARD

How can we create moments of awe in the lives of our students? Moments that will inspire them, enlighten and fuel their passion for learning. How can we give opportunities for our students to be elevated and to gain higher self awareness? These questions have been a central concern of mine for the last decade. The premise that there are others who feel similarly has led to my publishing this collection of essays.

The reader holding a book with a title as grand as this might be forgiven for being a little sceptical. I hope that you will forgive me if this is so. I hope you will find that this isn't a collection of simplistic cure-alls, barren models or lists of instructions mixed with know-it-all anecdote. It is simply a collection of my journal writings completed as opportunities for reflection arose during my time as a group instructor. My aim in publishing is to provide educators with inspiration and useful ideas to help them deliver high impact learning. It is my opinion that this can best be achieved when we also grasp the importance of the phenomenon of Awe. So the essays serve to share my understanding of how we can better provide opportunities for awesome moments in our students' learning experiences and to ensure their time with us will be rich in meaning and inspiration and even continue to be so long after they have left us.

"...to ensure their time with us will be rich in meaning and inspiration and even continue to be so long after they have left us."

PART ONE
A JOURNEY INTO AWESOMENESS

THE PRIMEVAL DAWN

Nature in its intense, impartial and ever-changing ways kept primitive man vigilant. The adaptability and resilience of our ancestors was the evolutionary hallmark of humanity. The intimacy with which they existed founded a personal connection with a 'holy earth' a belonging, a servant of nature, they coexisted.

Earth was both benevolent host and demonic ruler of their destiny. Through feast and famine roaming man learned that knowledge and skill were power. Time was not scarce. People were put first. The vastness provided perspective, it placed a small self in a big nature. To primitive man, awe was a daily occurrence. They were dwarfed by -

- The majesty of a starry expanse. Glorious sunsets.
- The oceans, waterfalls, wild beasts, beauties of nature.
- The mystery of birth and death.
- The storms and lightening, phenomena of terror.

Witnessing these overwhelming spectacles and the emotional response they invoked gave rise to an appreciation of the deep and mysterious world around them. It led to the telling of the first fables and myths. Through stories primitive man shared implicit values, bravery and virtuousness, suffering and kindness.

The premise of this book is that we too can rediscover some of our native capacity for awe and wonder. If only more of us could embrace the potential of awesomeness in our practice, we would address the very fulcrum of our contemporary lives.[1]

---

[1] Kirk J. Schneider (2008) Rediscovering Awe

The most beautiful emotion we can experience is the mysterious. It is the power of all true art and science. He to whom this emotion is a stranger, who can no longer pause to wonder and stand rapt in awe, is as good as dead.
Albert Einstein.

TREAD CAREFULLY

To see a world in a grain of sand
and a heaven in a wild flower.
To hold infinity in the palm of your hand
and eternity in an hour.
William Blake, from The Auguries of Innocence

Sometimes it might be meeting a great person. Sometimes it is through our being alone in wonder, other times it is when we are moved by great vastness and beauty, on other occasions when we encounter something so unfathomable that we are awed in the classical biblical sense. There are many different types of awesome experiences.

There are various ways to regard awe, we could be romantic, we could be idealistic, we could be self absorbed or perhaps we could be pragmatic. But whatever the manifestation, it pays to be mindful that to speak casually with others about such a personal and evocative emotion is to put it at risk of being extinguished. As W.B. Yates said, tread carefully as you tread on their dreams.

UNDERSTANDING AWE

"In the upper reaches of pleasure and on the boundary of fear is a little studied emotion - awe. Awe is felt about diverse events and objects, from waterfalls to childbirth to scenes of devastation. Fleeting and rare awe can change the course of a life in profound and permanent ways"
Keltner and Haidt [2]

People can fully understand what an awesome experience is without having some specific academic definition being provided to them.[3]

Seeing the grandeur or feeling the vastness of the environment; experiencing peacefulness, feeling a sense of authenticity and understanding, "sensing" the spiritual. It is an emotion that transcends culture or time - it is as old as human kind itself.

Early man depicted the feats of their great hunting lands on cave walls some 75,000 years ago, Plato wrote his thoughts on it 2300 years ago, Longinus wrote a treatise on it 2000 years ago,

---

[2] Keltner, Haidt (2003) Approaching awe, a moral, spiritual and aesthetic emotion, Cognition and Emotion 17(2) 297-314

[3] Coleman, T.C. (2014). Positive emotion in nature as a precursor to learning. International Journal of Education in Mathematics, Science and Technology, 2(3), 175-190

Emperor Huizong attempted to capture it in his paintings in the 11th Century. Leonardo Da Vinci was master of evoking it. Artists and Authors such as Chardin, Proust or Hugo championed awe in their work as revelation of something profound in the every day - the significance of the trivial things almost as an epiphany. All of these, and countless more, are testament to the enduring meaning of awe in our lives - each as they contemplated the world around them.

Despite this, you might be surprised to learn that it has proved difficult for psychologists to agree on a description of this remarkable emotion - in part because the triggers are so varied and the emotion's function unclear.[4] What exactly is a state of awe? Is it an elevation of mood, a rush of energy, a physical and mental lightness or a motivation, a freedom to imagine, to create and collaborate with colleagues?

Psychologist Abraham Maslow back in 1964 successfully demonstrated that the emotion of Awe is characteristic of *peak experiences*. In Maslow's study, he listed characteristic features of being "In Awe" as ego transcendence, otherness, perceptions of the world as good and beautiful, feeling receptive, humbled, fortunate, graced, transcended or resolved.

---

[4] (Lazarus :1991)

More recently, research has shown too that people associate Awe with inherently positive experiences only.[5] With this in mind, this study is concerned only with the concept of Awe that evokes positive experiences. The "Sublime" is however a broad concept which invokes more of terror and horror in its meaning (a fundamentally different type of experience to what we're interested in). As educators we shall refer (rightly or wrongly) to the sublime as a deep appreciative awareness and understanding- and the feeling of awe as those moments of emotional elevation, wonder, thrill and on occasion epiphany or revelation.

Scientists too have researched effects that may be associated with awe related states. Darwin cited certain facial actions, whilst others studied certain automated bodily states such as Goosebumps. And more recently, it's been shown that those Goosebumps may not be as arbitrary or spontaneous as we might imagine. "Awe is more of a mindset".[6] Research suggests you can cultivate Awe in similar ways, as

---

[5] Shiota, M. N., Keltner, D., & Mossman, A. (2007). The nature of awe: Elicitors, appraisals, and effects on self-concept. Cognition and Emotion, 21, 944-963.

[6] Rudd, M., Vohs, K., & Aaker, S. Awe Expands People's Perception of Time, Alters Decision Making, and Enhances Well-Being. Psychological Science.

you do gratefulness or happiness. Peak experiences, Maslow concludes, can bring about change in peoples identities and through meaningfulness and purpose a change in their 'spiritual' lives. The very personal nature of Awe should hopefully be apparent through the results of the experiments in the Appendix: our own meanings in our own words in our own worlds.

Yet for all of this I would hope that we might see more clearly a common theme that unites all people. Through the emotion of awe, we may find a rescaling of our concerns, transcendence of our differences and sharing our good fortune of being alive; that we will come to know the feeling that we all humbly share - the bond of *human compassion.*

AWE BASED COMPASSION

In my use of Compassion, I am attempting to address *that which brings us to action* - for others, the environment and ourselves. To clarify, compassion to me is:

- A benevolent inclination- not compunction.

- A moral law within- not from above;

- A defining aspect of humanity; selfless courage in purpose.

I believe we should aspire to be "strong poets". Where the poetry is in our living with compassion and grace and the strength is in bearing out life with nobility and acceptance. Gratitude is our balm. To live out one's life in another's vocabulary is a loss of reason. Reason should be ours – our life's purpose. This is the difference between a good life and a beautiful life.

THE HEART OF REVERENCE
By Dr Dachar Keltner[7]

"In caring and imagining the lives of others we encounter the fragile, fleeting beauty of life. This is the heart of reverence—our recognition that we are part of something sacred that is larger than any individual self...

The ancient Greeks believed that reverence—the feeling of awe for things that are greater than the self—is a critical substance of human communities, as important as our capacity for justice.

It is the feeling of reverence and awe that led Charles Darwin, standing in a South American forest, to muse, "It creates a feeling of wonder that so much beauty should be apparently created for so little purpose." Those feelings of awe spurred Darwin to imagine his theory of evolution by natural selection.

It was John Muir's feeling of awe at the idea that a black locust tree is from the pea family that led him to wander the United States and eventually find his way to the nearby Sierras. On one of his days there he wrote:

---

[7] *Dachar Keltner is professor of psychology at the University of California, Berkeley. He is also the author of* Born to Be Good: The Science of a Meaningful Life *and a co-editor of* The Compassionate Instinct: The Science of Human Goodness.

"We are now in the mountains and they are in us, kindling enthusiasm, making every nerve quiver, filling every pore and cell of us. Our flesh-and-bone tabernacle seems transparent as glass to the beauty about us, as if truly an inseparable part of it, thrilling with the air and trees, streams, and rocks, in the waves of the sun—a part of all nature, neither old nor young, sick nor well, but immortal."

And out of those experiences of awe Muir began to write and inspire others, and form the Sierra Club, and eventually inspire the creation of the state and national park system.

It is this sense of reverence that gives rise to the deep sense of gratitude and an appreciation of things that are given.

When scientists gave resources to people in 15 remote cultures, from the Amazon to Indonesia, they found that they gave on average 40 percent away to complete strangers. Adam Smith, the great economist, pondered why so much cooperation would arise in the England of the Industrial Revolution, when people were presumably driven by pure self interest. His answer: reverence and gratitude are the engines of healthy communities[8]."

---

[8] Keltner (2012) "Generation Wii… or Generation We?"

A CATALYST FOR CARING

Awe is an important emotion that may be regarded to have powerful implications for quality of life.[9] Today's students may be high achievers, but scratch the surface; you might find many will have no idea what for. This sense of meaninglessness is one of the main contributors to the high depression rates among our youth. Young people, in fact all of us, benefit from having a purpose in life - something meaningful to ourselves that also serves the "greater good".

In his book, *The Path to Purpose*, William Damon wrote of the immediate benefits from having purpose: In a series of studies of over 1,200 youth, aged 12 to 26, Damon found that those who were actively pursuing a clear purpose reaped tremendous benefits that were both immediate and that could also last a lifetime. Benefits such as an extra positive energy that not only kept students motivated to pursue their purpose, making them very strong learners, but opened them to positive emotions such as gratitude, self-confidence, optimism and a deep sense of fulfilment.

---

[9] Joel R. Agate & Whitney Ward, Awe as a Catalyst for Enhanced Outdoor Learning. , Southern Illinois University Carbondale

Kurt Hahn's emphasis on the pursuit of service to others similarly made mindful the vital need to contribute meaningfully to something worthwhile many years before. In his own words:

"I regard it as the foremost task of education to insure the survival of these qualities: an enterprising curiosity, an undefeatable spirit, tenacity in pursuit, readiness for sensible self denial, and above all, compassion"

"The passion of rescue reveals the highest dynamic of the human soul".

As an educator you can help your students discover a sense of purpose - by asking about what's most important to them and talking about one's own sense of purpose as an educator. To help someone begin a path to their life purpose may be one of the greatest services you could give.

Recent research suggests that you can help your students by facilitating experiences of awe. Many leisure researchers have identified the experience of awe in those engaged in outdoor and wilderness experiences.[10] Studies have also shown

---

[10] Heintzman, (2006)

that the experience of awe has the potential to turn students' lives in a new direction.[11] The new perspective of the world and our place in it makes us feel connected to something larger than ourselves - a crucial and necessary aspect of purpose. Imagine how life-changing this emotion could be for students who are struggling to find meaning in their lives and work. Awe has the potential to open minds to new ways of thinking, including what ones place in the world might be.

There have been recent calls for a renewal of awe and wonder as a means of developing a valuable and valued approach to environmental education.[12] A true exposure to nature may facilitate the awe that is needed to understand the world and the environment around us. The experience of awe towards a subject matter could inspire students and teachers to delve deeper and gain a greater understanding. A student who is fascinated by the vast wilderness may seek to gain a deeper knowledge, they might change habits and recycle, they might appreciate other wild spaces and be inclined to conserve.

---

[11] Dachar Keltner ref by Vicki Zakrzewski 2013 "How Awe Can Help Students Develop Purpose", http://greatergood.berkeley.edu/
[12] Ashley (2006)

Awe serves to drive the learning experience and improve the effectiveness of Educators.[13] We should make a conscious effort to bring awe into our practice so as to facilitate a love of learning and to broaden and deepen the skills of the learner[14].

---

[13] Myers, (2007)

[14] Schneider (2008)

"...a true exposure to nature may facilitate the awe that is needed to understand the world and the environment around us" (Ashley: 2006)

PART TWO

A PROPENSITY TO BE AWESTRUCK

AWE ELICITING EXPERIENCES

In attempting to orchestrate the emotion of awe we could quickly become accused of being engaged in a great folly. True, the complexity of people, their context and the perception of experiences are beyond the scope of this work, yet as I hope you find for yourself, it pays to engage with greatness and that despite appearances, it is an inherently human and natural phenomenon that we all share.

To support our efforts we should be clear what we are concerned with. Firstly, it is the positive aspect of the emotion that we are concerned with. Secondly, although positive, this does not necessarily mean it will always be a comfortable emotion to feel.

Think of those times when you were surprised in a way that challenged your comfortable mental structures, when you perhaps found yourselves in some resulting confusion or disorientation - this too is a symptom of the awesome. In this way awe sometimes leads us to become more enlightened[15].

---
[15] Keltner, D. Haidt, J. (2003)

In other words, awe can occur when facing a stimulus that is unaccounted for by current knowledge.

Awe can transform people and re-orientate their lives, their goals and values. Given the stability of personality and values, awe inducing events maybe one of the fastest and most powerful methods of personal change and growth.[16]

Broadly speaking we can say that Awe can be elicited by:
- Physical experiences
- Cognitive experiences
- Interpersonal experiences

Examples of some physical experiences could be accomplishing challenging feats, witnessing the mastery of others, working beyond one's own expectations, witnessing outstanding beauty. We can also feel awe when reliving a memory, reading a brief story or even watching a 60 second commercial. A small dose of awe can give participants a momentary boost in life satisfaction[17].

---

[16] John, O.P. & Srivastava, S (1999) The Big Five trait taxonomy: History, measurement, and theoretical perspectives. In LA Pervin & OP John (Eds.) Handbook of personality: Theory and research (pp 102-138)

In a review of the theoretical literature on awe, prominent researchers, Keltner and Haidt[18], proposed that awe-eliciting stimuli are characterised by two features: *perceptual vastness* and *need for accommodation*. Although the term "vastness" implies great physical size, in this usage "vast" describes any stimulus that challenges one's accustomed frame of reference in some dimension. A stimulus may convey vastness in physical space, in time, in number, in complexity of detail, in ability, even in volume of human experience. Vastness may be implied by a stimulus, rather than physically inherent in the stimulus. For example, one may experience a sense of vastness in a mathematical equation, not because the equation is literally long, but because of the vast number of observed physical processes it is able to explain and predict.

Be it the pleasure of solving a problem, the teamwork in rowing a cutter or the feeling of accomplishment on reaching a summit, experiences of awe stand "in the upper reaches of pleasure". Through outdoor adventure or pursuit of studies, this positive emotion of Awe may support significant and lasting change.

---

[17] Rudd, M., Vohs, K. and Aaker, J. (2012),
[18] Keltner and Haidt (2003)

"Moments of happiness...it isn't that we seize them, but that they seize us."
Ashley Montagu

RECIPROCITY & NATURE

"For the largest part of our species' existence, humans have negotiated relationships with every aspect of sensuous surroundings" David Abram.

In negotiating our relationship with our surroundings there is a balance of "give and take" to be struck. We are swayed by that which we are prepared to give.
In nature it becomes clear that we have to bring to it something of ourselves before we can begin to receive its nourishment.

> GIVE ATTENTION — OUR HEADS
> GIVE APPRECIATION — OUR HEARTS
> GIVE EFFORT — OUR HANDS

"In every faculty of human nature there is the urge to raise itself out of its state of lifelessness and clumsiness to the developed power which ... is in us" writes Pestalozzi in 'Swansong'[19].

Humans are tuned for relationship and for otherness. The eye wants to see, the ear wants to hear, the foot wants to walk and the hand wants to grasp. In the same

---

[19] Pestalozzi, J. H. (1826b). Pestalozzi's Sämmtliche Schriften: Volume 13 Schwanengesang [Swan Song]

way the heart wants to believe and to love, the mind wants to think.

Every child is born with natural powers and faculties and an instinctive urge to develop and grow.

THE POWER OF PLACE

There also exists a reciprocal relationship between us and the place we find ourselves. As visitors, we may give of ourselves to find a beauty, a resource or a perhaps some wisdom. A place recollected and shared may become a part of our personal story long after our journey has ended.

We give to the land a meaning that deepens our experiences. Though an experience might be fleeting, such as a surprise encounter with a wild animal, the place endures. The land keeps us in contact with ourselves.

This can be clearly seen if we look at the peoples whose bonds to the land are so close that it is part of their identity. The Aboriginal cultures of the world emphasize how the importance of place cannot be underestimated.

The Apache have a living landscape that they travel through merely by mentioning place names.

The Apache take great pleasure in reciting long lists of place names - succinct descriptions of the features to be found. Upon pronouncing or hearing such a name they would straight away feel themselves in the presence of that place. They experience themselves travelling in their minds, throughout the lands that they know. [20]

---

[20] Abram (1996)

PROP'S MAP

Journeys in the living land

In the dim lit Bothy we sat. Lindsay, the hut guardian, had been our host and poured us a dram from his bottle. Our "haggis and tatties" finished, Lindsay, spoke of his fond memories of being in the hills, of his days in Mountain Rescue and of his grandson, a bonny lad of 12, who because of his big size was known as "Prop".

It was Prop's story that I remember. When Lindsay was younger they both would go on long day hikes through the Cairngorms. They had their own personalised map, and spoke of places known only to them. When friends and family accompanied them they would visit intriguing and mysterious places.

Prop had his own names for the way-marks of their journey, Picnic Rock, Dipping Ford and the Laughing Stones were some of the stops. Each of the names on Props map recalled a happening or usefulness.

When Lindsay spoke of the journeys he had shared with Prop, when he spoke the names he was travelling back to those places; a stony outcrop of where he had shared great fun and laughter, the river in which he fell or the lunching spot. The hills were known as people – coloured with personality, some threatening, others hopeful - red head, black back, the sleeping twins.

When Lindsay spoke of those places on Props map he was alive as a child, animated, you could see the land reflected in his eyes.

With thanks to Lindsay Bryce, Hut Guardian, Glen Feshie Bothy.

EMOTION AND PURPOSE

"Hunger not to have, hunger to be" J.Dewey

It is said all emotion either rewards or punishes. In the original behaviourist model of emotion, it was argued that emotions are not chosen, but evoked as a conditioned response to stimuli (Watson, 1924). However, recent work challenges this popular view. Emotion also shows signs of being goal-directed processes. That is, they are at least partially in the realm of reward-governed behaviours, not conditioned responses; they are selected by their consequences, not their antecedents.

Emotion is still a reflex but it is ultimately *pulled by incentives rather than pushed by stimuli.* This is important - What is your goal? What is your purpose? Through meaning we begin to have a choice in our emotional life we begin to see a greater self.

At every point we construct new meanings in our lives. The starting point rests on our own shifting context – "needs means must" here we are uniquely on our own. Awe then affects us according to how we see the world - our map of reality and our purpose ... We might think we are sharing the same experience, yet, *in Awe, each of us are on our own.*

"You have two eyes, each consisting of 130 million photoreceptor cells. In each one of those cells, there are 100,000,000,000,000 (100 Trillion atoms) –
Each atom in each cell formed in the centre of a star, billions of years ago, and yet, here they are today, being utilized to capture the energy released from that same process.
All to expand the consciousness that is
YOU.
The universe has an interesting sense of irony, in that you are the universe experiencing itself – All you are is a thought."
Anonymous

THROUGH THE EYES OF A CHILD

"A child's world is fresh and new and beautiful, full of wonder and excitement"
Rachel Carson

The following extract is from "*Aesthetics and a Sense of Wonder*" by Ruth Wilson[21]:

Watch young children as it begins to snow or as they play in a pile of leaves. You'll witness an abundance of exuberance and joy.
You'll see children wholly engaged in the now, and you'll find them responding with their whole bodies.
They'll laugh, dance, run, listen, and perhaps even taste.
Adults, on the other hand, are more likely to respond with thoughts, spending little time immersing themselves in the moment.

---

[21] Dr Ruth Wilson is Author of Fostering a Sense of Wonder During the Early Childhood Years and Nature and Young Children.

Children's way of relating to the world corresponds to their unique way of knowing the world. A child's learning is dependent on concrete perceptual experiences. The wonder Rachel Carson[22] is referring to is a "true instinct for what is beautiful and awe inspiring" a "clear eyed vision."[23]

Children know the world — especially the natural environment — in a deep and direct manner. The type of knowing associated with wonder isn't primarily about thinking- it is something more intuitive than rational it is emotionally engaged and it involves a "direct knowing". [24] For children, the natural world is not a background or landscape for events, nor is it formal or abstract.[25]

We experience wonder as a spark inside of us — a spark which lights up our life and stirs our imagination. We also experience wonder as an emotion that takes us outside of ourselves and into a realm that is greater than ourselves. When strongly felt, this experience of "being outside of ourselves" — and outside of time — is sometimes referred to as ecstasy and is accompanied by intense joy or delight.[14]

---

[22] Rachael Carson, author of the "Silent Spring", the book that resulted in the use of the deadly pesticide, DDT, being outlawed in the USA and later by all other countries in the world.

[23] Carson (1956) p42.

[24] Hart (2005)

[25] Cobb (1977) & Sebba (1991).

To keep the spark of wonder burning in our daily lives, be mindful of how children experience wonder. They remain present in the now; they open all their senses to what they're experiencing; and they engage their hearts — not just their minds — as they experience and reflect on the world around them.

> *"Lift up the stone and you will find me,*
> *cleave the wood and I am there.*
> *He that wonders shall reign".*
>
> *(Oxyrynchus Paprus)*

HOLD ON TO THE MYSTERY

"Don't limit a child to your own learning, for he was born in another time." Tagore

The sense of wonder is much more pronounced in children than in adults[26]. What happens to us as we age? I can find no better explanation than the following extracts from Rabindranath Tagore's essay *"A Poet's School"*.

"From our very childhood habits are formed and knowledge is imparted in such a manner that our life is weaned away from nature and our mind and the world are set in opposition from the beginning of our days. Thus the greatest of educations for which we came prepared is neglected, and we are made to lose our world to find a bagful of information instead.

We rob the child of his earth to teach him geography, of language to teach him grammar. His hunger is for the Epic, but he is supplied with chronicles of facts and dates ... Child-nature protests against such calamity with all its power of suffering, subdued at last into silence by punishment."

---

[26] Carson (1956); Hart (2005).

As we grow, our understanding of the mysterious and uncertain world is refined; we become more certain in knowledge but at a cost. The processing of students through their time at school draws in their focus, channels their energies and changes their perception of reality- it is as if they leave with a pair of blinkers on with which they merely see what is known.

The race to find reliability in the world and safety from uncertainty comes with the cost of lost opportunities and losing sight of what is valid. This is something that leading corporations, business designers and innovators are becoming more and more aware of. The influential work of Roger Martin's[27] studies in innovation and corporate design proposes that there is a flow of understanding that each innovation passes. This consists of three phases; Mystery, Heuristic and Algorithm which he refers to as the "Knowledge Funnel". A modified version of his model is depicted in Figure 1 suggesting instead how a student understands the world changes as they go through the process of schooling.

At nursery, children explore and play. The world is full of mystery which is exciting and the

---

[27] Richard Martin (2009)"The Design of Business" Harvard Uni Press.

child's attention races from one thing to the next. There exists a special affinity and wonder for the natural environment.[28] "The child's direct ways of knowing and their interaction with the physical living world (e.g. rocks, trees, rain) is a sheer sensory experience."[29] The child's primary perception of a world which is fresh, unrepeatable and has a magic to it recedes over time.[30]

As children grow older patterns of understanding develop, knowledge is provided that enables children to focus on some things rather than others. They begin to extract out of a broad mysterious world the things that help them make sense of what they see. As schooling progresses they become students whose experience and knowledge begins to generate a narrower understanding - manageable rules of thumb. This is the move to the *Heuristic phase* of Martin's "Knowledge Funnel". Eventually the student moves to the *Algorithm phase* where they make such generalisations that their rules of thumb are converted to a fixed formula reducing the world from its complexity to one of evident simplicity, right and wrong, black and white.

---

[28] Ruth Wilson (1995), (2010)
[29] Edith Cobb (1977) pp. 28-29
[30] Sebba (1991) p. 398

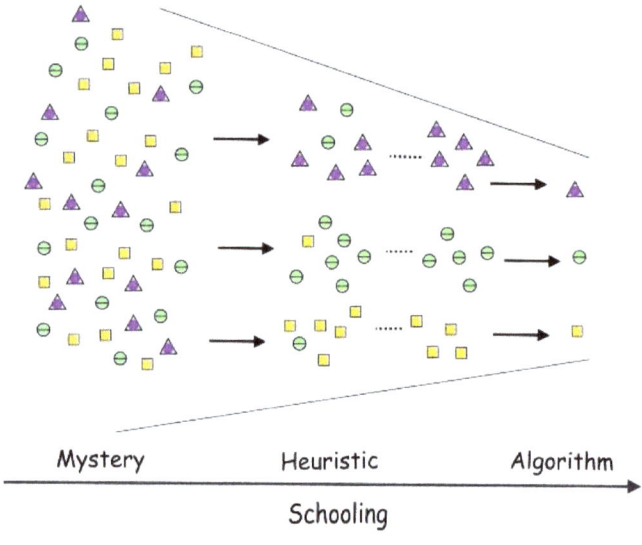

Fig 1: Becoming Blinkered: Education and The Knowledge Funnel.

This is symptomatic of something deeper found throughout the education establishment and society. We still apply an analytical approach to the world which has not changed from that proposed by Aristotle's famous work, *Analytica Posteriora* some 2400 years ago.

Aristotle himself warns the reader about the limitations of simplifying away the world into algorithms – simple rules, that today we could feed into a computer. In the last pages of his book he qualified that his thoughts were for the part of the world 'where things cannot be other than they are". Yes, we can be analytical of a tree or a rock but this alone is not seeing all of reality as it is. How can we weigh such things as our relationships, beliefs, values or inexplicable feelings? No amount of analysis will change the weather! We need to remove the blinkers. We create our problems by wanting things, or people, to be different.. I am not saying ignorance is bliss – but that sometimes deductive reasoning is not the only suitable form of thinking about the world. As Charles Sanders Peirce[31] said, "sometimes you've got to make a leap of the mind" to answer your question. "What's the best way I can understand what I see?" There are things in our environment that excite our curiosity but elude our understanding. Sometimes, it is best to appreciate the mystery and look beyond our blinkered concepts to see a bigger frame.

---

[31] Charles Sanders Peirce (1839–1914) was the founder of American pragmatism

"Two prisoners stare through bars, one sees mud the other sees stars"

The Garden gate.

© M. Leunig

RECEPTIVENESS TO EXPERIENCE

As educators, we must be mindfully supportive of our students' needs. It serves no purpose to conduct a review when your students are cold and hungry. Maslow famously proposed a Hierarchy of Needs. This Hierarchy serves as the bedrock of judgement when it comes to understanding the best time and place for learning. Our students open up and as they progress and develop through each layers of need. As the student is supported in their progression, they will be both collaboratively and personally engaged. Happily, they will grow in themselves.

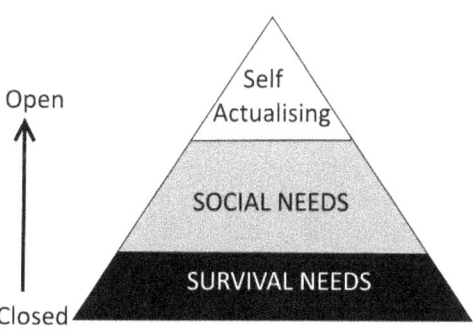

Fig 2.1: Student openness to learning and the Hierarchy of Needs

If only it was this easy! Although looking after the Survival Needs may seem self explanatory, (safety, food, shelter and warmth), there are other less clear dimensions to consider.

Firstly, Survival Needs are not only physical – they can be Psychological too. They come into play at any point and the most powerful means of evoking a student's shut down into survival mode is fear. This includes Perceived Fear. No matter how trivial or irrational a matter may seem to you, the response of a student is real. Fear might stem from a perceived threat from the group. Thus a student can move quickly from seeking assimilation into a closed defensive survival mode without any clear warning.

However, this also provides a great opportunity. For in stretching comfort zones we liberate students. Figure 2.2 depicts a curve that represents the receptiveness of people to experiences given their emotional state. Importantly it suggests a dip in receptiveness as students become more adamant about keeping within in their Comfort Zone.

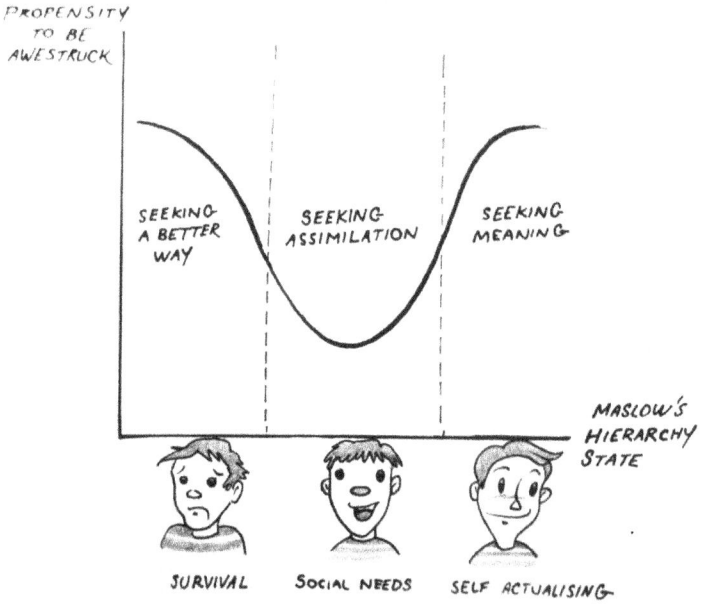

Figure 2.2: Propensity to be Awestruck

Our student's beliefs about themselves and their world have a profound impact on how they engage with challenge and seek support. Successfully dealing with the psychological dimension is as intrinsic to Maslow's Hierarchy as is shelter or food.

Perceived fear is itself a subtle matter that requires "unpeeling"...e.g. is it a fear of falling or a fear of humiliation? Where is the student focussing? – is it the opinion of themselves or that of others?

We all have the need for social assimilation - to be accepted – however our mindset will play a massive role in the way we achieve this, particularly in how we engage with those around us. A student with fixed beliefs about their ability may have learnt a complex set of strategies to protect them from feeling vulnerable[32]. If we do not address the fixed mindset of the student we leave them absorbed within their small self. The socially needy are not motivated to seek experiences that require revising their world view.

The social norms of urban modernity pervade every aspect of a young person's life. They adopt these norms unknowingly from all around them- but particularly from television. Many are positive, such as pluralism and egalitarianism, however many less so. Michael Foley proposed a set of modern norms as follows:[33]

- Righteousness of Entitlement
- Rejection of Difficulty
- The Glamour of Potential
- The Assault on Detachment
- The Undermining of Responsibility
- The Rejection of Difficulty
- A Loss of Transcendence

---

[32] See the work of Carol Dweck to fully appreciate the difference between Fixed and Growth Mindsets.

[33] Michael Foley (2010) The Age Of Absurdity: Why Modern Life Makes It Hard To Be Happy

The Passenger in our group is happy to coast along in their Comfort Zone and unquestionably accepts many of the social norms as their own – perhaps, even, they may seek to enforce them! They may outwardly be pro-social but it is as a means rather than in end in itself. Whilst busy assimilating they are less likely to be open to change. For now, they are happy to be *passengers* whose propensity to be awe struck is blinded. Without addressing their mindset, it would take a shock to wake them.

Figure2.2 suggests that there is a higher propensity to be Awestruck when we are receptive to change. The prisoner wants to be liberated. With a combination of progressive support and challenge we may free them from the thoughts and fears that keep them in their cell for one. Thus, paradoxically, the closed student who retreats within themselves may have a high propensity to be awe struck.

Lastly we have the student that, as an active participant, has grown to look and discover for them self. They happily engage with others with an open interest and sense of wonder that, in my opinion, makes them more likely be awe prone. Both the prisoner student and those students that participate fully in life are more awe prone simply because they are looking for better.

CULTIVATING AWEPRONENESS

"We come nearest to the great when we are great in humility." Rabi Tagore

There are different contexts for transformational moments – none as profound as our personal context – our body state.

We each receive something different from our surroundings according to the level of appreciation and awareness that we are prepared to give. I propose four generalised categories of Cultivated Awe in relation to the different transformational possibilities.

Here we move from considering what transformational moments exist to consider what possible outcomes we actually experience according to our current state. In every way we are part of a reciprocal relationship with nature. Figure 3 depicts a model which, in its attempt to categorise the different types of awesome experiences, may also help point to ways of cultivating the emotion. It has two axes. One moves from low levels of awareness to high levels of awareness. The other axis moves from low levels of appreciation to high levels of appreciation.

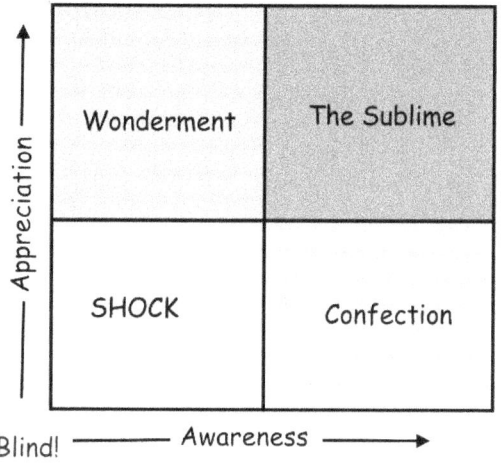

Fig.3: Categories of Awe

The combination of being highly aware and deeply appreciative is referred to here as "Seeing Deeply". The opposite is referred to as "Blind".
In this way we can examine how our personal context impels a different emotional experience. By choosing how we are, we select the outcome. Figure 3 simplifies Awe into the following four categories:

1. *Shock* and reconstruction that is not sought but challenges one's accustomed frame of reference in some dimension. Is this an act of God, like a Tsunami, or a shock how transient life is such as the sudden

death of a great person? Or is it the realisation of how unfit one is? The answer is entirely unique to the person. It might likely be the sudden realisation of the importance of something or someone we always took for granted.

2. *Wonderment* - a state of admiration or respect or gratefulness. It is enriching and lasting. Consider appreciating the rays of sunlight or the form of an acorn even!

3. *Confection* - a shallow realisation. What appears elaborately constructed is ultimately frivolous if there is no appreciation. Perhaps it might be feigned interest in another's delight, a self centred chance to profit, the rumour mill of another's life, or holding something so that others cannot share it. Ultimately confection is something that is unrewarding.

4. The *Sublime* (or vastness) – a moment of enlightenment or a peak experience that reignites purpose or augments ones world view. Perhaps this is in finding a "greater self" or the feeling of liberty when realising a life's purpose - seeing ourselves as part of something bigger than our own ego.

SATELLITES OF EMOTION

The following story is an example of how we each receive something different from our surroundings according to the level of appreciation and awareness that we are prepared to give.

-o0o-

It was clear and cold night. Despite being tired after a long day at the office, Chris was a-buzz; he had something exciting to share with Claire. Chris had just found out the exact time that the international Space Satellite would pass by that evening.

The prospect of witnessing and sharing this little special event filled him with excitement. That time was only minutes away. *"Come outside, come-on! come-on!"* he cheerfully implored. Claire slowly followed him out into the cold night and stood next to him in the darkness.

Looking up they saw the streak of silver draw quickly across the starry canvas- just below the Moon. *"Wow! There it is!"* Chris exclaimed in elation. *"Oh! Is that it?!"* replied Claire. The disparity in emotion between them couldn't have been greater.

Claire thought it was an inconvenient interruption. However, Chris was elated - moved by something so amazing it was hard to fathom. *"What do you mean an anti-climax?"*

"We just saw the ISS! The fact that, up there, 100km above us, hurtling around the earth at 20,000km per hour are two people sitting comfortably in a little silver foiled orb, playing with computers, conducting experiments, and perhaps even looking back at us. .. And here we are- looking back at them! knowing exactly when and where to look before they passed by! Don't you find that completely mind bogglingly awesome?"

Claire understood *"It must be a boy thing"* she smiled patiently.

-o0o-

Each of us, no matter how close, is still apart. We may view similar phenomena, but in our own very different ways. Our differing levels of awareness and appreciation can make the emotion of Awe an incredibly personal experience. At times it may seem like we are satellites of emotion.

PART THREE
THE FRAME FOR AWE

THE POWER OF CONTEXT

The choice of a word, the order it is spoken and when and where it is spoken all convey a context to the speaker's message. The interpretation can be framed and recalled based on your skill of placement. Your words and indeed the group's reactions are anchors to which memory clings to. They hold emotional cues and are easily recalled in an instant. As such these anchoring acts are very valuable if used positively. Their clever use will stir up emotion for time to come, long after the students have left you. In this way, the context and the meaning it anchors, becomes a powerful way to embed a shared purpose and openness to experience, in the hearts of students.

Place, learning processes and people all are components in anchoring an experience. They are part of the context. The context of our experiences also becomes a powerful anchor for our self concept and belief. For example, amongst big adventures we are immersed by big challenges and are absorbed into the experiences – then, when we move back to our everyday lives and encounter the many small things, we find them smaller in comparison and our adventurous experience seems bigger to us than the time we experienced it - AMPLIFIED by context. We have anchored ourselves to a bigger world, reprioritised what matters and opened up to greater possibilities. Transferring back to home life, the volume of our everyday challenges has been turned down - from mountains to mole hills - a transformation has taken place.

Anchoring & Circles' - Look at the centre circles, which looks bigger? In fact both inner circles are the same size. Anchoring is a powerful way to embed experiences into the memories of students. They are emotive memory builders

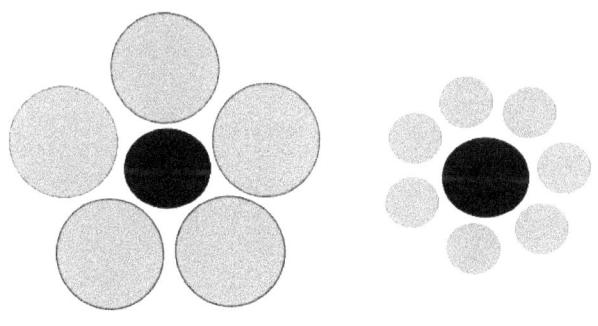

Fig 4: Comparative experiences

We have anchored ourselves to a bigger world, reprioritised to what matters and opened up to greater possibilities.

ADDRESS THE HEART

"If you want to build a ship, don't have people collect wood and assign tasks; Teach them to long for the sea"
Antoine De Saint Expury

"Two things fill the mind with ever new and increasing admiration and awe, the more often and steadily we reflect upon them: the starry heavens above me and the moral law within."
Immanuel Kant, Critique of Practical Reason.

We build and hold relationships on different levels. Behind it all, it is our values and beliefs that determine the way this is so. When as educators, our attention is drawn towards the judgement and behaviours of our students, do we find ourselves locked on the behaviours alone?

Our values and beliefs reinforce how events are given meaning and are at the core of our judgment and behaviours. To have the greatest impact the educator needs to dig deeper in order to reveal the values that their students hold. Is it a positive inclination to act or are we providing for a moral compulsion.

Why is it that the teacher finds out more about their students in five days on expedition than over the five years they share in the classroom? We all know how the busy pressurised agenda set for schools mean that it is difficult for teachers to authentically learn about the child on an individual basis. Then there is the limitation of the social contract between student and teacher - a contract that is predominantly based on results.

For all this, the outdoor educator has a great advantage over the in-class teacher. In particular:

- The different environment – shared context constraints and opportunities
- Group size has a massive impact on relationship:- Small groups are more personable; there is less time pressure, 1:1 interaction, better behaviour, more opportunities to understand behaviour more and see another side to the student.
- Time for more shared experience. Students get the opportunity to see you more as a human (or less depending on how you are!)Space for personal example and positive inclination as opposed to the school rules and imposed obligations:

The most fundamental level of influence on our relationships and interactions is the shared environment (i.e., when and where the relationships within the group take place). Environmental factors determine the context and constraints under which people will engage with the world. More so, when that environment is one of wild space and interaction with nature- there is so much to gain.

The student's relationship with their environment can be a rich area to explore values. In supporting a student to progress in their sense of care and responsibility for the natural environment we also ask of them to reflect on their ways of relating to the world, how they value themselves and others too.

ENGAGING WITH THE ENVIRONMENT

*"When we engage with nature,
we engage with human nature*

The relationship with our environment is one that varies from person to person and within the individual over time.

At one end, our relationship with the natural environment is completely alien. Here the individual is busily living a life that completely ignorant of nature and its benefits –the world for them is a place of technology, convenience food, cityscapes and purpose under the shadow of industry. From this extreme there exists a series of steps where the relationship between the individual and nature changes and eventually deepens.

Nick Rhys, at The Outward Bound Trust, developed a simple model which represents the different types of relationships with Nature. The Rhys Six Box Model detailed here clearly identifies six different ways of understanding and relating to the Natural Environment. For the outdoor educator this presents a values based framework which can guide strategy in facilitating environmental engagement.

Fig 5: The Rhys Six Box Model: Ways of Relating to the Natural Environment

1.	**Ignorant** of the natural Environment
2.	The natural environment is **Alien** (Dangerous scary, dirty)
3.	**Exploiting** the natural environment
4.	**Adventure** in the natural Environment
5.	**Interdependent** with the natural environment
6.	**Transformative.**

The use of immersion helps students to address their existing concept of nature. The use of adventure learning opens up opportunities for growth. The use of transient art and music develops bonds of inter relationship[34]. Solo experiences, appreciation exercises and the bringing to attention moves our hearts towards moments of deep insight.

It is wonderful for groups to share together how their relationship with nature has been changed by their experience. This reflective exercise is as

---

[34] E.g. Weintraub, L. (2012) To Life! Eco Art in Pursuit of a Sustainable Planet Berkeley, CA: Uni of California Press

simple as having your group stand at a starting point (at one of the 6 Boxes), and then ask them to walk to where they now feel their relationship with the natural environment is at the end of their time with you.

As the student moves towards a more interdependent relationship with their world they open up the frequency of opportunities to be awed more frequently – through regular appreciative wonderments. The scope for planning orchestrated activities widens as the individual's relationship with the natural environment develops. Their appreciation could be supported with the acquisition of skills, knowledge, responsibilities and respect. Through self directed adventure and challenge the students might look back upon their "Wow! Moments" and perhaps see how they personally have been changed by the experience.

The Rhys Six Box Model is an important environmental model for the both the educator and the students to assess their developing relationship with the world around them. It provides a context for understanding which intervention would have a greater impact. The model also parallels the categorisation of Awe – moving from experiences of Shock in an "Alien world" to the wonderment and sublime moments of Deep Vision where the individual recognises they are an intrinsic part of something much greater.

The model is non judgemental – it simply clarifies and delineates between a set of different possible relationships that exist. In this way it supports a focus on positively engaging with the natural environment regardless of where one is. We may move between the boxes on different occasions and importantly with different levels of new found appreciation. Ignorance, then, rather than being seen negatively may result from a profound realisation of how little one understands.

"There is no single or set "nature" either as "the natural world" or "the nature of things."
The greatest respect we can pay to nature is not to trap it, but to acknowledge that it eludes us and that our own nature is also fluid, open, and conditional."
Gary Snyder

DEFAMILIARISATION – SEEING WITH NEW EYES

"Our accustomed way of seeing is just one way, yet as it hardens through habit, it tends to become our only way. To see the world anew is of a piece with wisdom." Henry Shukman

Defamiliarisation is the technique of making the familiar seems strange so that our students experience something in a new way, from a new angle, and gain a new understanding of it[35]. As far as the technique of defamiliarisation wakes students us up from being on auto-pilot, it helps provide for awe in our experiences.

As an emotion, awe ignites imagination and expands our horizons: This waking up demonstrates the epiphanic quality awe can have when it strips us of our limited views, of what we think we know. The questioning of assumptions about something as fundamental as our sense of self can bring about a radical new openness. When we find that the

---

[35] The term "defamiliarisation" was coined by Russian critic and writer Viktor Schklovsky in his 1925 essay "Art as Technique"

assumptions or pre conceptions were wrong our world is enriched and broadened - like finding a whole new ocean.

Making the familiar strange is perhaps not as hard as it seems.

- Talk about motivations for why the students did things, how they felt when certain things happened, moments when they feel mistrust or doubt. Get others in the group to see others story from a new perspective by creating opportunities for them to listen and share the groups different views.

- Through challenge and support the educator can provide opportunities for individuals to achieve that which they thought was impossible, that they feared, to challenge deep set beliefs that have perhaps held them back.

- Lastly, when two phenomena are brought together by unexpected likeness such as with a Metaphor, both are "made strange." Metaphor provides another angle with which to understand. Metaphor is always a matter of defamiliarisation. The mountain and lakes, the journeys bring new ways of relating to life.

Effective learning transfer brings the students own world into perspective. Being close to the wilderness and finding a relatable meaning revives the student's appreciation of their home life. It helps them to discover a renewed purpose – to see again as if for the first time.

> *"The real voyage of discovery consists not in seeking new landscapes, but in having new eyes."*
> — *Marcel Proust*

FRAMING AND AWE BASED LEARNING

"Precept without concept is blind"
Immanuel Kant

You may have heard of the saying about the path to hell being strewn with good intentions. Despite the best wishes and enthusiasm, pressing a child to walk, cycle or row for a time is an unhappy experience waiting to happen.

Indeed many a path *is* strewn with good intentions. How would you react if being forced to put effort in for unknown time or destination, given no information or mis-information and not being permitted to stop? Yet this is this not an uncommon experience of many a family outing? Merely for the want of a purpose; how quickly can all the good be undone!

When we share a common goal we become more equal. When we share an understanding we motivate. When we take time to inform we respect and when we challenge by choice we engage. If you understand this then you understand the building blocks for successful Framing.

Framing is simply relating experiences that will be present during the session to the students' everyday life. You can often change persons 'frame' just by changing their emotional state. Just as metaphor describes one thing in terms of something totally unrelated in order to bring meaning or a unique perspective, the process of framing brings a personal dimension to learning- it brings a focus.

Using students own world experiences or using a story as a metaphor you open up a whole new world of learning possibilities which can bring imagery to mind and prime points of view. Perhaps most importantly, you create a shared meaning in the group –it builds a common understanding.

As an example: One could start a climbing activity by asking your students *"How did you learn to walk? ... Did you read a book?!"* By going over the story of how a baby learns to walk we have framed a challenge with a focus on resilience in learning or the growth mindset. The frame supports the students with a purpose and provides a base for them to reflect on *"Trying and not quitting after the first go"* in other aspects of their life too.

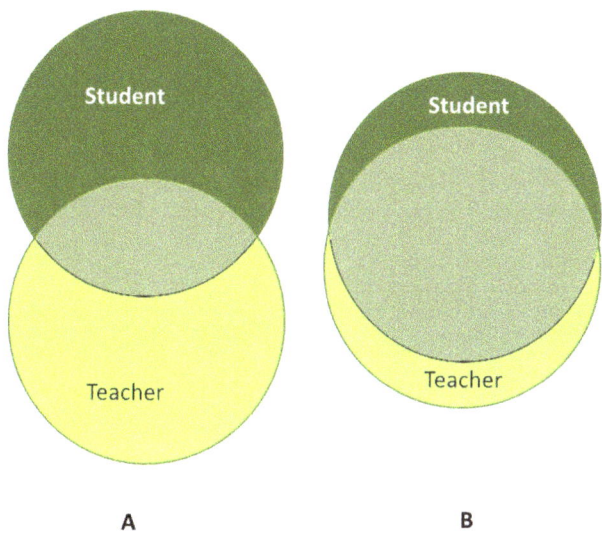

Fig 6: Schema Model – To Frame is to share understanding

Using the Schema Model we can represent framing as an aligning of two different sets of experience. To frame is to align the shared purpose between a student and their teacher.

Framing an experience provides an opportunity for students to personalise an experience through a shared context you have given them. The greater choice of the activity is then cropped by the frame they employ. It is given a shared purpose and a personal meaning, relevant context from which they can construct meaning through their interaction. For these reasons, Framing is a crucial component in a social learning experience. Framing an activity is critical if the student is to transfer any lasting learning to their own life.

Framing breathes life into a task, personalises and changes it emotionally. Relating experiences from the student's everyday life to the learning creates a shared context. It is essential.

> *"We do not learn by our experience but by our capacity for experience"* Siddhārtha Gautama

METAPHOR- PRIMING FOR AWE

Framing personalises and changes a task emotionally and breathes life into an activity by making it relevant to a student's own life. Relating experiences from the student's everyday lives to the learning creates a shared context and is essential. If people have no concept of what you are on about then your efforts to frame are wasted.

Metaphors are powerful. Their use in framing is an important foundation in priming your students with awe creating potential. Simply by describing one thing in terms of something totally unrelated opens up a world of rich possibilities - permitting us to see the extra ordinary in the ordinary.

Just as the process of framing brings a personal dimension to learning; the metaphor brings meaning or a unique perspective to our communication

One way we can frame the world around us is to create stories about it. When faced with complex situations, a story picks out the key elements and its metaphor brings the student a fuller understanding. The following story "Building a Cathedral"[36] is an example of how framing an activity brings purpose.

---

[36]From Greg Coker " Building Cathedrals: The Power of Purpose"

PERCEPTION & THE ART OF BUILDING CATHEDRALS

It's not so much what we do but the purpose that we see that can make for happy and engaged life. The following is a well known teaching story for helping people see the importance of what they do. It highlights the importance of understanding the bigger picture and can help team members appreciate everyone's role and value their team's goal more fully.

One day in 1671, Christopher Wren observed three bricklayers on a scaffold, one crouched, one half-standing and one standing very tall, working very hard and fast.
He asked the first bricklayer, "What are you doing?"
"I'm laying bricks," the first bricklayer said.
The man asked the second bricklayer the same question.
"I'm putting up a wall," was the reply.
The passerby then posed the question to the third bricklayer.
"What are you doing?" he asked.
"I'm building a great cathedral," the third bricklayer replied. "

Are you laying bricks or are you building a Cathedral?

To further this example of metaphor, the use of "a Cathedral" can be used to help people understand relationships and values. E.g. On criticism: *"It's a bit like a person looking at a cathedral and seeing only its bricks"*

Raymond Carver was a powerful story teller. Of his work, his own personal favourite involved the metaphor of a cathedral. In the story the cathedral is the subject of the conversation between a blind man and a jealous husband - the story's narrator.

Carver used the cathedral as a powerful metaphor for the spiritual awakening the narrator needed; to look at people as individuals; to look from a different point of view.

Through the story we see how the narrator's eyes are opened metaphorically through the insight of the blind man. The narrator learns reluctantly that seeing is more than a visual experience, it's seeing with your mind and heart as well.

Raymond Carver (1983)" Cathedral" published by Vintage Classics 2009

SUCCESSFUL OUTCOMES

Despite our best efforts, the impact of interventions can vary widely depending on the students chosen level of participation. An educator attempting to orchestrate a group culture that is receptive to the more vulnerable emotions has to accept that the outcomes are not always as anticipated. A pinch of reality helps every one - control typically rests within the group

The complexity of people is such that priming students prior to a suitable activity is of great importance for transferring learning into their lives. Even if it is as simple as your choice of place, a change in spoken volume or link to their last activity. *The skill of connecting with your students grows as you grow as a person*.

Successful outcomes of an activity may be a personal reflection or a change in a student's perspective. In particular, it is Peak Experiences that may open students up to a sense of vastness and will turn the student *outside* of themselves. Gratitude too makes us more aware of others.

The importance of Framing however is its ability to provide a student with a context for transferring their learning back to their own life as they are participating in the activity. Those experiences which are tied back into the meaning of personal life are the takeaways –the transfer of learning.

The impact of our approach and the degree to which the participant is *turned* outward or inward results in a range of beneficial outcomes. This is depicted in the Figure 7.

Framing & Transfer

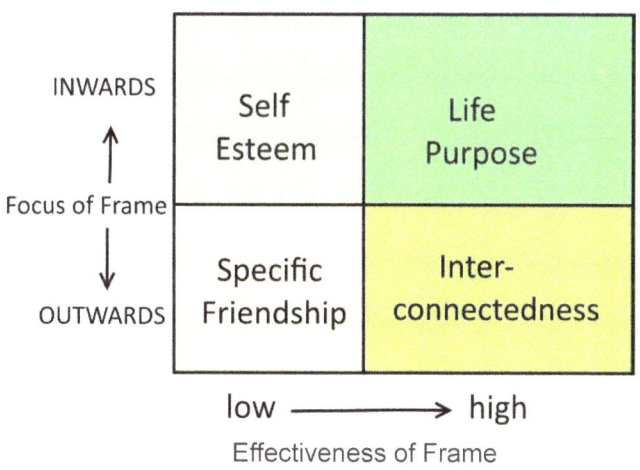

Fig 7: Effectiveness of an instructor's framing

Turning a student outwards to their social context may lead them to find a deeper level of interconnectedness. The student may make specific enduring friendships or on deeper impact occasions they find place for an active social interest and service in their goals.

Alternatively, some experiences may turn students inwards to a deeper level of reflection and self awareness. This might be useful in bolstering self esteem, however deep impact experiences may themselves be where they find a purpose or mission in life. Such encounters are highly engaging and emotional and form a transformative encounter.

"What do you do with the extrovert?' 'I turn him outside in,' was the reply. 'And with the introvert?' 'I turn him inside out.'
Kurt Hahn

PART FOUR

MAGIC MOMENTS

AN AWESCAPE

When Momentous and Significant come together... it is Magnificent:

What is wonderful about the energy of an awesome experience is that it can be drawn upon when the event is recalled. Awe can be recreated in the mind, even manufactured.

A key idea is that awe 'lives beyond' the moment - it develops and grows and can be recalled instantly. Awe can be relived again and again. There is an inner "AweScape."

Louise Chawla (1990) once noted, the spaces and views which we experience as children become inner landscapes or "Ecstatic memories" which then remain with us. These "ecstatic memories" and the positive emotion associated with them do not have to be something we experience only as children. Magic moments can be experienced at any age and remain with us "like radioactive jewels buried within us, emitting energy across the years of our life" (Chawla, 1990, p. 18).

It would seem that taking the time to share our personal experiences of a "magic moment" would be a very valuable way of anchoring positive emotions to a student's emotional state.

I have conducted a dialogue with dozens of people and groups questioning them about those moments in their lives that they would describe as "Magic Moments". The resulting answers were depicted in a diagram I refer to as an "AweScape".

Of all the possible peak experiences that could be encountered, it is those with personal meaning that are recalled – the awesome moments. So I would ask repeatedly until they could no longer recall any more! In groups, students were asked to recall one magic moment each – surprisingly, the result was a similar depiction to that of an individual. There was little or no mention of significant materialistic purchases.

Figure 8 is an example of an AweScape diagram. Complicated and varied it shows that we deeply value what is magnificent and augment these moments to our concept of self. The process of thinking about experiences changes the emotional state at that very moment -just through recollecting a memory.

Using the Awescape as a reflective exercise - get your students to draw out each other's moments of awe. The moments depicted are affirmations or acknowledgements of what is meaningful in life. Such moments are now a gift to be shared with each other.

The AweScape is just a depiction of the peak moments of one's life's' past. It is a timed activity to help people to reflect and appreciate. And in doing so, they would be able to relate the value of that experience on a deeper level.

Everyone has awesome experiences at some level or another. Maybe not everybody is aware of them. But if they reflect upon their experiences then they would become more aware of their "jewel like" value in everyday life.

The AweScape is not a one off exercise and its purpose is not merely to change an emotional state, but also to help people savour and to think about life in a way that sees things more positively, more optimistic and inspired.

Reflecting through the awesome moments of one's own life itself inspires awe. The magic of the moment lives on.

ENCOUNTERS WITH AWESOMENESS

During each AweScape exercise conducted with students a lot of experiences were collected. Of these recollections were reoccurring themes that came through involving the awe eliciting elements of physical, emotional and cognitive experience.

Research supports the idea that awe in the outdoors may be facilitated by the *things one sees*; *the things one does*; or by ones *individual characteristics*. (Agate: 2010). However in classifying in these general terms we perhaps run the risk of being blinkered by oversimplification mentioned in Part 2 (see Hold onto the Mystery).

Magic moments relate to moments that involved some of the following themes, many were a combination of them:

1. Achievement
2. Life Events
3. Relationships
4. Environmental Exposure
5. Moments of Appreciation
6. Grand Nature

The drawing in Fig. 8 is an example of an AweScape which depicts Magic Moments, some of which are a combination of these themes. (e.g. getting engaged on top of Mount Kilimanjaro would be a combination of an Achievement, Environmental Exposure and a Life Event). More generally the varying types of Awe can be seen to engage aspects of Self, Social, Natural and "Classical" elements as follows:

- **Self** - finding awe from your own achievements e.g. graduating, giving birth. There are many ways to find awe in your 'self' if you know where to look. As an instructor it is essential to facilitate/direct people to reflect on their progress/problems.
- **Social** - finding awe from sharing experiences with others. In the AweScape above this comes from working with students, sharing the same goal towards success It may also be entirely personal e.g. snorkelling with a significant other, making memories to last a lifetime.
- **Natural** - finding awe from nature, seeing the beauty of our world, being/feeling part of it. From watching a sunset, to climbing a mountain and walking above the clouds. From being caught out

in an electric thunderstorm to the silence of snowfall. Feeling part of nature can remind us that there is something much greater than ourselves & make some of our problems/obstacles seem somewhat smaller.

- **Classical Awe (Myth)** – Classical awe suggests a greater agency is involved. The power and the great vastness moves us as in the primitive or biblical sense. We feel a bigger presence, we engage with that which we do not understand. Myth results from the tendency to seek an explanation for a phenomenon what we have no answers for. In the great uncertainties we find security and purpose through having faith in our beliefs.

Figure 9 is an attempt to simplify the varying types of Awe eliciting experiences gathered through life. It can be seen to engage aspects of Self, Social, Natural and "Classical" elements. The point here is no matter what our backgrounds are, we all have some archetypal experiences in common- experiences that we all can relate to. From our Peak experiences in life we are able to relive our feelings of awe – our lives can be enriched long after the experience. Through reflection we are all able to share our sense of wonder with each other.

Figure 9: From Peak Experiences to Awe

EVOLVING THEMES OF AWE

As our understanding of the world changes so too does our relationship with the natural world. Throughout the evolution of human society we have developed an increasing sophistication of language and thought which has tempered our ways of seeing the world.

The different families of experiences can be seen as continuum of states which parallel our development in material and knowledge. Although the following essay shares a broad human history of thought, it must be emphasised we each have our own parallel mindset. The following is as much a statement on the individual's own relationship with the awesome in their world as that of their society.

| Ignorant | Powerful Alien | Romantic | Self | Interdependence |

Fig. 10: Evolving themes of Awe

In the last 60 years, mankind has developed more knowledge and gained more control over its environment than at any point in its existence. Our relationship with the world has changed significantly.

The evolving themes of Awe reflect an evolution of meaning. Though our encounters of awe and wonder due to ignorance and fear may not be as common as they were with our ancestors; who does not fill with adrenalin when witnessing fork lightening rip across the sky? It is in our biology.

That same storm 1000 years ago would certainly seem more sinister and foreboding. The dogma of a totalitarian religion and the brutality of its laws and rituals that today seem barbaric were (*and still are*) a response to the powerlessness of people. They framed a world in myth and agency to explain away the uncertainty and address people's fears. We still live in myth, it might seem to be very different, but look beyond the power of celebrity, and passion for fame and you will see the same elemental desires for agency or validation. This is the Classical type of awe - where power was incarnate, the wrath of nature was a consequence and its blessings an endless resource to be ruthlessly exploited and conquered.

During the Greek and Roman enlightenments, a flourishing of the arts and thinking about beauty paved the way for a new emphasis, one that was aesthetic and appreciative and one which was only rediscovered over a thousand years later. The Western Enlightenment that followed, amongst other things, embraced aesthetics[37] in a way that led to a more secularised relationship with our world. Edmund Burke's and Immanuel Kant's philosophical enquiry into the Sublime and Beautiful in the 18th Century were of enormous importance in creating a move from a Classic to Romantic view of the world – moving from the supernatural to the natural. Eventually the power and abundance of nature became valued for its transcending beauty alone.[38] Romantic artist's thinkers and poets began to see nobility in wild nature. The poets and painters depicted a world where we would be awed by the sublime beauty[39]. The outdoors became somewhere to go for restorative healing.

In much more recent times, since the advent of the sixties, and its youth's longing for liberation, an emphasis on self grew. The Beat Generation took 'The Road' as its metaphor for finding purpose in the journey. In refusing to adopt social norms, individuals saw themselves as their own heroic narrator in life - in awe of their potential to change and be changed.

---

[37] Aesthetics" the faculty by which we discern beauty, is derived from the Greek word for "senses

[38] Diderot, Voltaire, and Rousseau's libertine writings made headway that later romanticists such as Wordsworth & Byron would embrace.

[39] E. g. Burke's " passion caused by the great and sublime in nature"

Technology too has changed our relationship with the outdoors. The automobile and plane have made transport to remote places - that was once unimaginably difficult – quick, safe and comfortable; we have become adventurers in search of achievement, fascinated with firsts and record breakers, of great personal experiences in the big world. The need for meaning and purpose has provided modern man with a place to lose and find themselves again.

Lastly there is a sphere where, through globalisation of communications, contagion of finance, disease, global warming we have become more aware of our interdependence with nature, nations and our neighbours. We are awed by the great social feats of collaborative effort of say putting a man on the moon. But perhaps more importantly, beyond such anthropomorphist views, we are become moved by our being part of and caring for a greater entity, our planet. Through a deepening of perspective[40] we are awed by our mere existence.

---

[40] Consider Carl Sagan's '"Pale Blue Dot" or the deep ecology of Arne Naess.

ON THE LIKELIHOOD OF ELICITORS

As Outdoor Educator's with Outward Bound® it is our job to facilitate peak learning and frontier adventure to unlock the potential of the young people that visit us. We will be seen as amongst the gatekeepers to such big experiences. So how often are we likely to come by an experience that transformational in some way? Is it often?

Simply put, it depends. It depends on us, it depends on our students and it depends on the learning space (or milieu). The *opportunities* for awe eliciting events are as much a personal fact as the measured probability of an occurrence. After all, we generally see what we are mindful of and this is in turn formed by our needs.

Figure 11 suggests relative frequency of awe eliciting experiences. Some are more accessible than others. Its triangle form suggests that there is a difference in the frequency of different awe eliciting experiences. It also suggests that the chance of encountering such elicitors changes as the relationship with our world changes.

Each level is a category of Awe, as formulated in the earlier essay titled *Encounters with Awesomeness*. Running alongside each level is an equivalent evolving theme (or a mindset) of how a person interprets their world.

It is proposed that occasions for encountering Awe happen a lot more often with shared experiences (e.g. in challenge and adventure) than coming into contact with some special phenomenon. Awesome full day adventures can and do result in a great likelihood of transformational learning. The likelihood for Awe eliciting experiences thus grows when the capacity of experiences moves into our own hands. As educators, this must be of great interest to us.

Fig 11: Relative Frequency of awe eliciting experiences

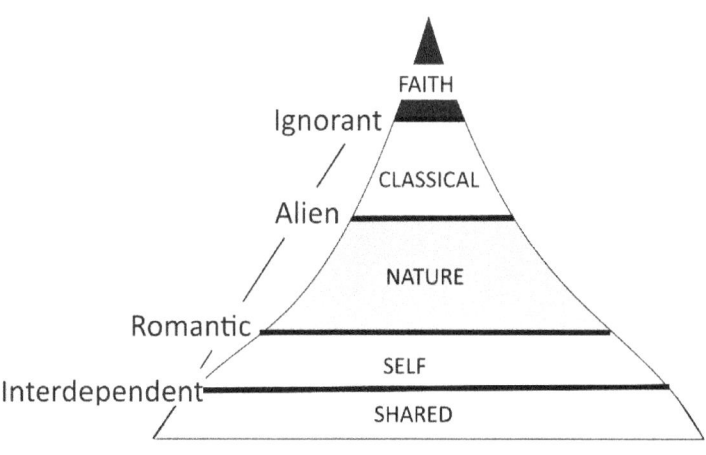

Importantly, this apparent hierarchy is not such. It should not be inferred that there is a difference in the *value* of experiences – that, like beauty, is in the eye of the beholder. There is a value too in scarcity. Take the example of "Faith" – its importance transcends every level of life and yet the personal epiphany or inspiration behind it is not common at all. Whatever Faith means to a person, consciously or not, becomes part of their life; a fabric of values and meanings created to account for the dissonance of unresolved issues and sufferings that arise in life. Profound "Road to Damascus" experiences are an example of such occasions. In times of distress, that which explains and provides a satisfactory resolution and purpose is deeply life changing. They are gifts.

When we support our students to move from ignorance, from seeing their world as threatening (or Alien) or move them from a sense of entitlement or narcissism, we become high impact educators.

In providing the right space for learning our students will become more mindful of their potential and, with a deepened appreciation of their interdependence, they may perhaps be moved to see their world and their place in it, in a more compassionate and positive light.

The Vastness - Some experiences encompass all classifications of awe

PART FIVE

TRANSFORMATIVE LEARNING

INTERPRETATION OF UNIQUE MOMENTS

To answer a doubt
all knowledge goes out
A riddle or a crickets cry
Is to a doubt a good reply.
Blake

Awe lends itself to reconstruction: - Unique moments have different meaning to each of us - we weave them into our individual biography. Whilst meaning making in the construction of our biography is important it should still be left to each of us individually to make our own connections. Any outside directive input that offers interpretation will minimize the development of the story in the learner's context.

To enhance the re constructive process and to encourage students to make new meaning it is important that the educator stays at the periphery. This is hard. However, if we were to direct the process through diagnosis of problems and formulating our own solutions for the students we rob them of deep learning opportunities. We take away important unique moments and outcomes

An educator who sees themselves as an untouchable expert may typically foist an opinion upon students from their own adult world. It is no surprise then that such an educator will place great value their own input yet, through their intervention, act to marginalise young people experiences. As such, they repeatedly fail in assisting the individual to explore their own potential for change. Any awe elicited is coincidental from the educator's efforts - stemming from rare physical and classical encounters and with meaning being constructed through antithesis.

To help students with their "meaning making" it is important to refuse the invitation to engage in a directive encounter that may tell things about the instructor rather than the student. To that end we should honour the students own ability to make meaning themselves, in their terms and from their context rather than from our "higher" perspective. To be able to say I don't know to the simplest of questions in a disarming and unpretentious manner quickly teaches the students to have confidence and trust their own decision making.

"THE THING"

A playful mystery & What's in a Name

Amongst the highlands there is a small set of islands, were children visit each summer for adventure and fun. Over their stay the students would learn to survive and cook for themselves, they would climb and sea kayak and do all the great adventures that many adventure camps offer. Yet there was one activity that could be found nowhere else. At night, when it was the right time, the students had the opportunity to complete an obstacle course known as "The Thing".

Not quite knowing what to expect, the students would psyche each other up to see who would go first. To have to complete an obstacle course called The Thing was no mean feat. Of course to help them, the instructors would allay the student's fears by saying that it is not the worst...they know of other courses that are worse... Like "The Horror" or if they survive that they could travel to another island to attempt "The IT".

Over, under and through, mud, cargo netting and "ghosts". All the students survived – their memories will come alive with the mention of these names forever more.

There were intriguing mysteries too. From their arrival to their departure the leaders would forewarn students about the Tale of the Old Lady. So terrible were the happenings that they were not allowed to say. The students, intrigued by this are unable to let it go, till the last day they asked each instructor repeatedly, seeking to know. They never did find out.

I am indebted to Rich Hill for sharing his experience and this example of using suspense and imagination to heighten perceived adventure.

TRANSFORMATIVE LEARNING

"Only through contact with the bigger picture can we provide potential to transform"

In developing our understanding of the world we assimilate experiences and the wisdom of countless others before us. Through this process our world view adjusts to more accurately reflect reality.

When we encounter something that does not fit with our understanding, we feel uncomfortable and this dissonance impels us to find a solution. Sometimes that solution is found through assimilating the experience with our current understanding, however other times the experience itself changes us.

Piaget described both these outcomes as assimilative experiences and accommodative experiences (Piaget 1954)

It is important to make a clear distinction between the two outcomes. When we assimilate we are adding to our existing knowledge and this is an informative learning process. But when the experience changes us we are encountering transformational learning. The process of being transformed by an experience is referred to as accommodation.

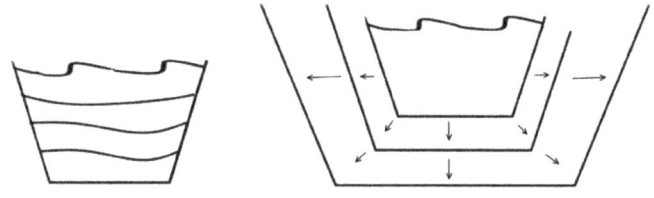

Fig 12: Informative process v transformational process

Accommodation involves the process of adjusting mental structures that cannot be assimilated with existing experience (Piaget & Inhelder 1966/69). What is critical is that the stimulus dramatically expands the observer's usual frame of reference in some way. Like a bucket being made bigger rather than being filled up. The informative process of providing knowledge just adds to an individual's existing understanding- it doesn't change them it is assimilated and forgotten. As an Outdoor Educator it is our role to facilitate experiences that can lead to positive lasting change. To this end we should be clear on what it is we are looking to achieve – the beneficial outcome - and understand the reasons behind it. To bring people to transformative moments requires a holistic *and* authentic strategy aligned with our own values. We should try to understand the frame we want to develop from the intervention and the consequence of the outcome for sustained growth... not just meddle with session based tactics.

A JOURNEY WITHIN

"'Every time I describe a city I am saying something about Venice."
Italo Calvino– Invisible Cities

The mind recreates memories over time and models their meaning to suit current personal experiences. This is important to know as what is experienced now is not the same as what is remembered tomorrow. People have a tendency to remould. What was a miserable cold wet experience on the mountain may be recalled later as a liberating wild adventure. The memory that constructs Awe will not be a carbon copy with reality of the experience. The best lessons develop through reflection and time.

Nobel Laureate, Daniel Kahneman, proposed the thesis that each of us has two selves. There are two versions of you - The Experiencing Self and the Remembering Self. Each is a reflection of who you are, yet each focus on different things. The memory of an experience is what we keep from our living. It is our remembering self that guides our choices.

Khaneman says "We cannot think of any circumstance that affects our [happiness] without it distorting its importance" An example is of a person sharing a story about a concert they went to which had great music but how the whole performance was ruined because there was a terrible screeching sound at the end. Despite the 40 minutes of wonderful music, they were left with a memory of how it was ruined. What was ruined was not the experience, but the memory of the experience. *What we remember is a weighted average of the Peak Experience and End Experience* - Everything else pails into insignificance. Understanding this is of enormous importance to our practice as facilitators. Get it right and the rain, the hardship and the cold will all be forgotten, leaving only the great achievements and peak experiences to mould their future choices.

What was a miserable cold wet experience on the mountain may be recalled later as a liberating wild adventure!

THE MAP IS NOT THE TERRITORY

We all have an understanding of the world around us. It is not an exact picture; it is a bit like a map that represents the actual territory - the real world. This map is known as our World View or Schema. It is what we base our decisions and behaviours on. So a lot depends on the accuracy of our map, our world view.

The two Venn diagrams depicted in Figure 13 represent the world view of two people. The first diagram represents the world view of someone who has an accurate map of reality. This overlap represents what they correctly understand, what is congruent with the world around and the world inside their head. This person's self concept is aligned with reality.

The second Venn diagram shows a much smaller overlap between schema and reality. This represents a person with an incongruent world view. The person whose self concept is not aligned with reality will encounter more disruption, stress and misunderstanding in their lives. The incongruity constantly challenges their own identity, questions the inner schema that they base their decisions on and leads to more frequent occasions of confusion and discomfort.

Fig 13: Rogers' Personality Structure

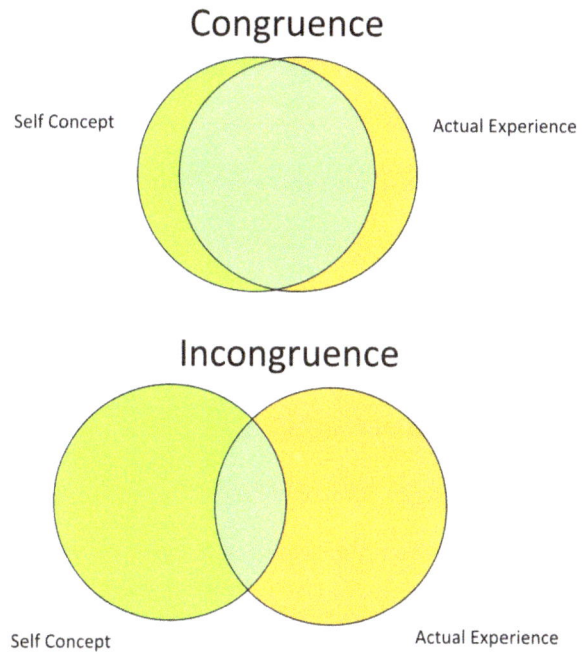

It is not only the learning needs which are explicit, but the student also has a need to develop their understanding of the world around them and themselves. In achieving this they will be learning from observing your own attitudes, values and behaviours as much as your planned session.

In our work as facilitators we are helping young people find themselves - each transformative moment of Awe works to redraw the map slightly and helps them to find their way.

WHAT ARE YOU REALLY TEACHING?

Here is a check list for you to consider before getting too deep into the ideas in this book. If you read only one part, let it be this one. There is no point in progressing any further if the following do not chime with your practice. Be sure to get the basic right fist - ask yourself -what is it that are you really teaching?

- Your example is everything; watch your language, thoughts and actions. Students will adopt your biases and opinions even if you are not teaching them. So beware of your language and remember inaction is an action. What you don't say matters as much as what you do, so be vigilant to challenge inappropriate behaviour. Things said in those small

conversations have a massive impact on students.
- The educator makes his/her relation with the child through what he/she is - which depends on their thoughts on the world.
- 'Immediacy' is important in the educator - student relationship. Students do not learn from educator's they dislike or that they think do not like them. Smile! Psychological, physical closeness is increased with an educator's level of enthusiasm or passion. Use their names, listen! Your passion has a positive impact on students[41].
- Respect must be earned! Equality of the Educator and student. You lose 'Gravitas' but you gain 'Voice' in their learning.
- Self awareness and self knowledge are key components of emotional intelligence.
- Educators who involve their students in meaningful ways with the world around them increase their students learning. They must know what is meaningful to their students and to know their students better they must *listen to them*.

---

[41] Carbonneau, Vallerand, Fernet and Guay (2008)

- Do you appreciate the importance of
    - the role of emotions in focusing attention,
    - the importance of first hand experiences
    - building personal meaning from the student's point of view? [42]

MEMORY AND THE EFFECT OF FRAME

"Time and memory are true artists: they remould reality closer to the heart's desire" John Dewey

The memory of an experience is what we keep from our living experience. It is unique to us and it changes each time it is recalled, gradually modified by our context. It is our remembering self that guides our choices.

This is not new. Back in the 1930's, Frederic Bartlett was conducting influential experiments into memory. His experiments showed how memory recollection is a type of reproduction that develops

---
[42] Biggs (1996)

many changes from the original experience. In remembering, some parts of the reproduction are subtracted, others are embellished, and still others become additions that were completely new. In effect, the participants had built new stories upon the ruins of the original memory. Each little distortion in the participants' memory becomes part of the fabric when the memory is next recalled.

Numerous experiments document Bartlett's claim that memories for events are strongly affected by the framework of prior knowledge in terms of which they are understood. By asking participants to take on a certain view point or to relate to a particular place in their life, we evoke a powerful frame prior to their experience

In one study, participants were asked to take one of two different viewpoints: that of a prospective homebuyer or that of a burglar. They were then asked to read a description of a family home.

The different perspectives affected what was later remembered. In the case of the 'home buyers' it was, a leaky roof. In the case of the 'burglars' it was a valuable coin collection[43].

---

[43] *Anderson and Pichert,(1978).*

Such experiments demonstrate how, participants' memory is affected by their knowledge of the world. We fit our particular recollections into general outlines or Schemas, filling in various gaps in memory without knowing that we do so.

THE EXPERIENCING SELF

Nothing matters so much as much as when you think about it. What we bring our attention impacts our experiences. The experiencing self is how you feel right now. The role of our attention is central to what we experience. Consider someone in love who is stuck in a traffic jam, how they experience this as opposed to someone who is depressed. The role of attention is central to endogenous happiness – the well being that comes from our living and immediate thinking about it.

A large study of US and French women on how they spent their day showed that they both spent approximately the same amount of time eating. However they were significantly different in well being measures, with the French being happier. The difference was that the French women spent more of that time focusing on eating than their American counterparts.

We live an anticipated memory. Part of our species extraordinary abilities is its ability to commit complicated tasks to unconscious pre programmed skills. (Take driving a car for example). For our experiencing self however, this means that giving ones attention to a moment is not as easy as it seems. It is a skill to master. Our attention then, is hampered by our mind's rush to commit experiences to existing gestalt groupings and to commit new tasks to unconsciousness. To be aware is to see. We must wake up to the immediate moment.

It is the same with our interaction with the natural environment. Our students may be too into themselves to see the migrating geese fly by in-formation or to hear them encourage each other with their honks. If we are consumed with ourselves we will never see the light shimmering of the ripples, reflect the spectrum of colours, or cast mysterious shadows. Underwhelmed by ourselves we live underwhelmed by the little wonders of the world.

Similarly, attempts to capture everything and chronologise it into online timelines takes us away from being more fully mindful in the moment and withdraws some of that gratefulness of just being with

the temporal moment. True, our memory is fallible, but how can the fumbling efforts to capture a photograph on our smart phone compare to the full engagement with a personally significant moment captured by an immediacy that can never be repeated.

We have to get outdoors. Out there! With our feet on the ground, inhaling the air, we have to be physically in contact with the world. We will not get the mystery of life looking at digitally reproduced images on-line. Awe emanates from within us. Awe helps us experience life from a different perspective – a bigger frame, an appreciative focus - and opens up new ways in how to see ourselves, others and the environment. Through wonderment we feel our own inherent value of just being.

"Happiness cannot be travelled to, owned, earned, or consumed. Happiness is the spiritual experience of living every moment with love and gratitude." David Waitley

THE BEAUTY OF IMPERFECTION

"What we see changes what we know. What we know changes what we see" Jean Piaget.

The world around us is beautiful but it is not perfect. Consider the butterfly emerging from its chrysalis with its crumpled wings – little does it know it has provided us with a gift. Unable to feed or defend itself against dangers it allows us to make connections with what we know and with our personal experiences. Not yet capable of flying, the little creature's vulnerability might remind us that we too are born with our own challenges. Perhaps in our different appearances, aloneness, poverty, or other differences, we might paint the world as cruel.

Yet, in this imperfection there is a deep beauty, unknowable to us – that perhaps leads us to realize sincere compassion. Just by being brought to realize this, we add to the world. Is this not what is truly awe inspiring, and sufficient reason for our vocation. Is it not our struggle that makes us more?

To facilitate such moments for your students, whether delicate or bounding, is to "say" to them: live deeply, never quit and in time you too will fly".

APPENDIX

THE LABORATORY OF AWE

The following three experiments are ways for you to explore the uniquely personal nature of Awe.

Using these activities with your group will hopefully help in facilitating a greater understanding in the importance of individual differences and recognise that the creation of personal experience is something more of an art form than a prescribed recipe.

The result will hopefully make the ideas expressed in these essays more useful in your practice.

Experiment I: Group Reflection
Experiment II: Word Association
Experiment III: Camouflage

Experiment I: Group Reflections

By collecting together the experiences of a group you will find that they can be put into different categories relating to self, place, shared emotion, achievement and time.

1) Ask the students to write their own definition of Awe. Discuss in pairs. Across the group facilitate the sharing of each other's ideas.
2) Ask students to think of a time in their life when they felt this Awe. "Picture in your mind". Share in pairs, Share across the group and get them to contribute to depicting a group AweScape.
3) List a positive moment in your life that you would consider had some impact upon who you are today.
4) What similarities (or differences) exist between this moment and your definition of Awe.

Experiment II: Word Association

The construction of meaning highlights the personal nature of learning. We should aspire to facilitate. Some would say we should simply provide stimulus, provide space and guide, rather than tell. If only it were that simple! For your own view of the world is a totally different construction to that of your students. The fact that they even understand you is astonishing. The following experiment will help explain.

With a group of people, ask them to gather in with pen and paper and write down the words that they associate with something that you will give them. Instructions:

"In a moment I am going to say a word."
"I want you to write down as many words as you can that you associate with that word".
"Are you ready? ... "
    '"DOG"

15 seconds later ask them to stop...

Experiment II: Cont'd

Have the group give estimates of how many of their words they think that *everyone* else in the room will also have written. Two, three, four?

Get a student to read out their list, and then word by word ask people in the room to put their hand up if they have that word. How many times did *everybody* put their hand up?

No brain is the same. Indeed, the structure of the nervous system accounts for the happy fact that we each have our own and only our own experiences.

Experiment III: Camouflage

Question A) what do you see in this picture? If you see nothing - keep looking.

Question B) if you see 'something' then try to see 'nothing' - can you do this?

So too is the sense that we make from the chaotic world around us. Once we construct and order it, it is very difficult for it to be unseen. This world view is called a *Schema*. The Dalmatian once seen cannot be unseen.

We construct order from chaos and find it incredibly difficult if not impossible to un-see order. 'Unseeing the Dalmatians' is impossible. Our Schema is the filter that we see the world through and once we encounter a phenomenon that is outside that order we have a 'paradigm shift' and we must reorganise our whole life to establish a new understanding. This is an important high impact outcome of being awestruck.

ACKNOWLEDGEMENTS

In writing, one seems to speak alone, but this is an illusion. There have been many who have been instrumental to the writing of these essays. This is the product of many good people and occasions and some not so good. For those who have seen me at my best and worst and wisely spoken; thank you.

In particular, I am indebted to those who have been my mentors and whose quality of thought has always been a source of ignition. In particular to Nick Austin, Tim Deighton and Neal Anderson who have kindly supported me on my journey as a reflective practitioner with their inspirational ideas, stories and searching dialogue. I am immensely grateful for Dr Dacher Keltner, Dr Ruth Wilson, the wonderful artist Michael Leunig and my inspirational colleague Nick Rhys for the permission to use their work. I thank my talented illustrator, Christian Kirasic for his work.

I am grateful for the exceptional vision, inspiration and encouragement of the Directors at The

Outward Bound Trust UK. I cannot emphasis enough how indebted we all for the leadership and direction Kim Parry, Will Ripley and of Nick Barrett, in their stewardship of the Trust's mission.

Thanks also to my esteemed colleagues from The Outward Bound Trust's Ullswater and Aberdovey Centres, particularly those who supported my progression as an instructor in some way - you know who you are! I thank colleagues, such as Justin Hale, Kim Collison, Gary Fitzgerald and Rich Hill for their friendship, good humour and for being bastions of authenticity in an industry prone to attracting deified egos. I am also grateful for those who have at one point or another shared their thoughtful insights, ideas and stories with me: Andrew Dziemian – on the Sublime whilst canoeing, Chris Davies on the Satellites of emotion, Rebecca Hind on a student letter of Awe, Kate O'Brien on mindsets, to Sarah Lowe on sharing some great books and to Andy Hewett on his discussion of empathy.

I am especially indebted to those who gave a lot of their time and attention to carefully critique and check my writing, particularly to Mary and Michael Long.

My dear long suffering wife Sarah, thank you for always believing in me, loving me and putting up with my long absences whilst I was overseas, on the road or working in the Lake District.

I thank the reader for whom, in their generosity, I hope will forgive me for any omission, error or contradiction for which I am solely accountable. I am grateful for their time and any thought which may be taken to inform their own practice. It is their word that matters and will attest to whatever value this work holds in time.

Kevin Long
August 2014

REFERENCES

Abram, David (1996) The Spell of the Sensuous Vintage Press p155.

Adler, M. G. & Fagley, N. S. (2005). Appreciation: Individual differences in finding value and meaning as a unique predictor of subjective well-being. Journal of Personality, 73(1), 79-114.

Agate, Joel, (2010). "Inspiring Awe in the Outdoors: A Mechanistic and Functional Analysis" PhD Dissertations. Paper 607.

Agate J R., Ward W, (2012) [1] Awe as a Catalyst for Enhanced Outdoor Learning Southern Illinois University Carbondale. Coalition for Education in the Outdoors Eleventh Biennial Research Symposium

Anderson, R.C., and Pichert, J. 1978. Recall of previously unrecallable information following a shift in perspective. Journal of Verbal Learning and Verbal Behavior 17:1-12.

Ashley, M. (2006). Finding the right kind of awe and wonder: The metaphysical potential of religion to ground an environmental ethic. Canadian Journal of Environmental Education, 11, 88-99.

Averill, J., Stanat, P., & More, T. (1998). Aesthetics and the environment. Review of General Psychology, 2, 153-174.

Burkhard,Vern (February 6, 2011). "Diving Into Mysteries" IdeaConnection Interview with Roger Martin, Press
http://www.ideaconnection.com/open-innovation-articles/00237-Diving-Into-Mysteries.html

Bono, G., Emmons, R.A., Mc Cullough, M. (2004) "Gratitude in practice and the practice of gratitude" in p464 "Positive Psychology in Practice" Linley P.A. (2004) John Wiley & Sons: New York
Bower, G.H.; Black, J.B; and Turner, T.J. 1979. Scripts in memory for texts. Cognitive Psychology 11:177-220

Biggs, J. (1996) "Enhancing teaching through constructive alignment" Higher Education 32: 347-364, 1996

Burke, Edmund (1756) "A Philosophical Enquiry into the Origin of Our Ideas of the Sublime and Beautiful"

Carbonneau, N., Vallerand, R. J., Fernet, C., & Guay, F. (2008). The role of passion for teaching in intrapersonal and interpersonal consequences. Journal of Educational Psychology, 4, 977-987.
Carson, R. (1956). The sense of wonder. New York: Harper & Row.

Chawla, L. (1990). Ecstatic places. Children's Environments Quarterly, 7(4), 18-23.

Coleman, T.C. (2014). Positive emotion in nature as a precursor to learning. International Journal of Education in Mathematics, Science and Technology, 2(3), 175-190

Cobb, E. (1977). The ecology of imagination in childhood. New York: Columbia University Press.

Coker, G. (2012)" Building Cathedrals: The Power of Purpose"
http://www.thecathedralinstitute.com/2012/05/13/the-recovering-bricklayer/

Csikszentmihalyi M (1998) The flow experience and its significance for human psychology. Cambridge University Press. pp. 15-35

Damon, W (2008) *The Path to Purpose: Helping our children find their calling in life.* New York: Free Press

de Saint-Exupéry, A. (1943). The Little Prince. Orlando: Harcourt Books.

Dewey J. (1920) "Reconstruction in Philosophy" Henry Holt & CO. : New York

Emmons, R. A. (2007) "Thanks!" Boston: Ma; Houghton – Mifflin

Emmons R.A. Mishra, A. (2010) "Why gratitude enhances wellbeing"
http://psychology.ucdavis.edu/Labs/PWT/Image/emmons/file/16_Sheldon_Chapter-16-1%5B1%5D.pdf

Halstead, J. & Halstead, A. (2004). Awe, tragedy and the human condition. International Journal of Children's Spirituality, 9(2), 163-175

Hart, T. (2005). Spiritual experiences and capacities of children and youth. In E. C. Rhehlkepartain, P. E. King, l. Wagener,and P. L. Benson (Eds.). The Handbook of Spiritual Development in Childhood and Adolescence, pp. 163-178. Thousand Oaks: Sage Publications

Heintzman, P. (2006). Men's wilderness experience and spirituality: A qualitative study. Northeastern recreation research symposium.

Heschel, A. (1983). I asked for wonder. Chestnut Ridge, NY: Crossroad Publishing.

Johnson, B. (2002). On the spiritual benefits of wilderness. International Journal of Wilderness, 8(3), 28-32.

Jarvis, P. (2012) "Learning to be a person in society" Ch2 in Contemporary Theories of Learning, Knud Illeris (2009), Routledge. P26.

John, O.P. & Srivastava, S (1999) The Big Five trait taxonomy: History, measurement, and theoretical perspectives. In LA Pervin & OP John (Eds.) Handbook of personality: Theory and research (pp 102-138) New York: Guilford Press.

Kant, I (1764) Observations on the Feeling of the Beautiful and Sublime

Keats, J. Ode on a Grecian Urn. http://www.bartleby.com/101/625.html (retrieved January 22, 2010).

Kemple, K. M., & Johnson, C. A. (2002). From the inside out: Nurturing aesthetic response to nature in the primary grades. Childhood Education, 78(4) (retrieved online May, 23, 2009).

Keltner, Haidt (2003) Approaching awe, a moral, spiritual and aesthetic emotion , Cognition and Emotion 17(2) 297-314

Keltner, D. (2009). Born to be good: The science of a meaningful life. New York: W. W. Norton & Company.

Keltner (2012) "Generation Wii… or Generation We?" Graduation Address, University of California, Berkeley. *http://greatergood.berkeley.edu/*

Kirk J. Schneider Rediscovering Awe: A New Front in Humanistic

Psychology, Psychotherapy, and Societ, Canadian Journal of Counselling / Revue canadienne de counseling / 2008, Vol. 42:1 67

Lazarus, R. (1991). "Cognition and Motivation in Emotion," American Psychologist, 46: 362–67.

LeDoux, J., (1998). The Emotional Brain: The Mysterious Underpinnings of Emotional Life, New York: Simon and Schuster.

Martin, Roger L. (Nov 2009). *The Design of Business*. Harvard Business

Mezirow (2000) "Learning as Transformation: Critical Perspectives on a Theory in Progress" San Francisco: Jossey Bass

Pestalozzi, J. H. (1826b). Pestalozzi's sämmtliche Schriften: Volume 13 Schwanengesang [Swan song]. Stuttgart, Germany: Cotta
http://babel.hathitrust.org

Phillipe Narval, (2011) The Aristocracy of Service- The legacy of Kurt Hahn in the 21 st Century" Uni Oxford, MSc Disertation.

Proust M, *(1923) "Remembrance of Things Past; Vol. V, _The Captive" Ch. II (1929 C. K. Scott Moncrieff translation)

Rorty, R. (1997) "Achieving our Country" Cambridge MA: Harvard Uni Press

Rudd, M., Vohs, K., & Aaker, S. (2012). Awe Expands People's Perception of Time, Alters Decision Making, and Enhances Well-Being. Psychological Science.

Rumi, J. (1997). The essential Rumi. San Francisco: HarperOne.

Schneider, (2008) Rediscovering Awe: A New Front in
Humanistic Psychology, Psychotherapy, and Society
Canadian Journal of Counselling / Revue canadienne de counseling / 2008, Vol. 42:1 67

Schklovsky, V. (1925) "Art as Technique" http://web.fmk.edu.rs/files/blogs/2010-11/MI/Misliti_film/Viktor_Sklovski_Art_as_Technique.pdf

Sebba, R. (1991). The landscapes of childhood — The reflection of childhood's environment in adult memories and in children's attitudes. Environment and Behavior, 23(4), 395-422.

Seligman, M. & Csikszentmihalyi, M. (2000). Positive Psychology: An Introduction. *American Psychologist, January, 2000.* 55(1): 5-14

Shiota, M. N., Keltner, D., & Mossman, A. (2007). The nature of awe: Elicitors, appraisals, and effects on self-concept. Cognition and Emotion, 21, 944-963.

Wilson, R. A. (2008). Nature and young children — encouraging creative play and learning in natural environments. London: Routledge.

Zakrzewski V. (2013) "How Awe Can Help Students Develop Purpose", http://greatergood.berkeley.edu/

INDEX

A

Abram, David, 23
accommodation, 21
accommodative experiences, 97
Achievement, 80
anchor, 52
anchors, 52
Apache, 25
appreciation, 3, 23, 46, 49
assimilative experiences, 97
attention 23, 108, 109
attitudes, 103
authentic, 98
awe eliciting, 80, 88
AweScape, 78

B

Bartlett, 106, 107
beauty, 5, 20, 24, 81, 90, 112
Benefits, 13
biography, 93
Blake, 5, 93
blind, 47

C

Carson, Rachel, 31 32, 33, 35
Chardin, 7
Child-nature, 35
children, 31, 32, 33, 35, 77, 95

choice, 29, 52, 65, 67, 72
coincidental, 94
compassion, 9, 14, 112, 123
concept of self, 78
confection, 48
confusion, 19, 102
construct new meanings, 29
context, 19, 29, 46, 47, 52, 60, 66, 67, 69, 73, 74, 93, 94, 106

D

Damon, William, 13
defamiliarisation, 62, 63
Dewey, 29, 99, 106
direct knowing, 32
dissonance, 97

E

educator, 14, 72, 93, 94
Educators, 16
Einstein, 4
emotional cues, 52
endogenous happiness, 108
engaged, 15, 19, 31, 32, 41, 81
enlightenment, 48
environmental education, 15
epiphany, 7, 8, 90
evolution, 2
experience, 4- 8, 15,24, 29, 32, 37, 46-48, 52, 60-67, 77, 80, 97- 100, 106, 110, 127

uniqueness, 119
experiencing self, 108

F

facilitate, 15, 16, 17, 81, 98, 113
facilitating, 14
framing, 67
Framing, iii, v, 65, 66, 69, 73

G

Gestalt grouping, 109
goosebumps, 8
gratefulness, 9, 109
gratitude, 14, 111
growth, 24, 72

H

Haidt, J, 6, 20, 21, 127
Hahn, Kurt, 14, 74, 128
Happiness, 111
heart, 24, 99, 106
Hierarchy of Needs, v, 41
high impact learning, vii

I

impact, vii, 72, 73, 74, 108, 120
Informative process, 98
instructor, vi, 81, 94, 96, 123

K

Kant, Immanuel, 65

Kahneman, Daniel, 99
Keltner, Dacher, 6, 8, 20, 21, 127, 129

L

learner, 16
learning, vi, vii, 6, 16, 32, 35, 52, 66, 68, 69, 73, 94, 97, 118, 126
learning processes, 52
life, 6, 13, 14, 15, 20, 29, 32, 35, 53, 66, 68, 69, 73, 74, 77, 90, 107, 117, 120

M

Magic moments, 77, 80
Magic Moments, 78
Maslow, 7, 9, 41
meaning making, 94
memory, 20, 52, 53, 78, 99, 100, 106, 108, 109, 110, 125
Metaphor, iii, 63, 69
mindful, 5, 14, 33, 109
mountains, 53 81, 99, 101
Muir, 11, 12
mystery, 2, 95
Myth, 90

N

natural world, 32

O

optimism, 13, 79, *see positive*
otherness, 7, 23

outcomes, 46, 72, 74, 97
Outward Bound, 7, ii, 58, 122, 123

P

paradigm shif, 120
participant, 45, 73
participation, 72
passengers, 45
peak experiences, 7, 9
perspective, 15, 63, 66, 69, 72, 87, 94, 110, 125
perspectives, 107
Pestalozzi, 23
physical, 7, 20, 21, 80, 94
Piaget, 97, 98, 112
Place names, 24
Positive, 8, 13, 19, 21, 55, 61, 77, 90, 98
potential, 3, 15, 69, 94, 97
priming, 69, 72
primitive, 2, 3, 82
Proust, 7
purpose, 9, 13, 14, 15, 29, 48, 52, 65, 67, 74, 90

R

Rachel Carson, 31-35
relationship, 23
relationship with nature, 46
Remembering Self, 99

S

Schema, 102, 120
Seeing Deeply, 47
self awareness, vi, 74
Seneca, 6
stories, 3, 69, 107, 122
Snyder, Gary, 61

T

Tagore, 35, 46
transfer of learning, 73
transferring learning, 72
transformational process, 98
transformative, 74, 98, 104

U

unconscious, 109

V

vastness, 2, 5, 6, 21, 48, 72
vocation, 112
vulnerability, 112

W

well being, 108
wild, 24, 58, 86
wilderness, 14, 24, 64, 127
Wilson, Ruth, 31
wonder, 3- 5, 8, 15, 31- 33, 35
wonderment, 110
World View, 102

> **The Outward Bound Trust** gives you the opportunity to practically demonstrate leadership and team work skills in very real situations, helping you to build a foundation for a future career.
>
> **Professor Nicholas Gair,**
> **Visiting Professor, Leeds Beckett University**

LOOK TO YOUR FUTURE

outwardbound.org.uk/individuals

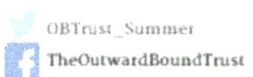

OBTrust_Summer
TheOutwardBoundTrust

THE OUTWARD BOUND TRUST

*Proceeds from the sale of this book
will be used to support young people attending the
Outward Bound Trust's Award*

www.ingramcontent.com/pod-product-compliance
Lightning Source LLC
Chambersburg PA
CBHW040321300426
44112CB00020B/2835